The New Mail-Order Marriage -A True Story of the K-1 Fiancé Visa

Navigating Long Distance Relationships in the Digital Age: Including Info for LGBT Relationships & Advice for Older Singles

By

Callie Cooper-Sato

Copyright © 2020 – **Streets of Dream Press**

All Rights Reserved.

No part of this publication may be reproduced, stored in a retrieval system or transmitted in any form or by any means, electronic, mechanical, photocopying, recording or otherwise without the proper written consent of the copyright holder, except brief quotations used in a review.\

Published by:

Streets of Dream Press

Cover & Interior designed

By

Renee Leadsman

First Edition

Contents

Meeting Your Soulmate 6

Legalities of International Relationships 15

    Marriage Fraud 17

    Fiancé Visa 18

    Immigration Support 21

    After the Wedding 22

Precautions to Take 25

    Qualities That Should Raise Suspicion 28

    There's Still Hope! 30

A Match Made in Heaven 33

    Marriage Brokers 33

    Check the Legitimacy of an Agency 36

    International Matchmaking Services 37

Navigating the International Singles World 38

    My Story 39

    My Advice 41

Challenges of Long-Distance Courtship 44

    Overcoming Rumors and Prejudice 46

    Decisions to Make 49

Planning the Big Day! 54

    Make Lists! 56

    Blending Traditions 57

    Pushing the Budget 58

Overseas LGBT Couples 62

    The Legalities 63

    LGBT Dating Sites 65

    Safety Concerns 67

    Don't Give Up! 68

    Barriers 69

    Victories 72

Advice for the Older Single 74

    Precautions 76

    Tips 77

Appendix A: Immigration Lawyers 79

Appendix B: Dating Sites 82

Appendix C: Wedding Planners 88

Appendix D: Foreign Matchmaking Services 90

Appendix E: Resources for Support 93

Appendix F: LBGTQ Dating Sites 95

Appendix G: LGBT Advocacy Groups 99

Appendix H: Dating Sites for the Older Single 103

Conclusion..105

Meeting Your Soulmate

We met quickly, frequently chatting hour – on – the - hour and went on our first date as soon as I could get him into the United States.

I picked the time and the place for our initial acquaintance. I chose a local restaurant adjacent to a hotel with a lounge where a crowd of people gathered.

It would be the perfect location.

I wasn't taking any chances in case he turned out to be a pervert. I was nervous and absolutely filled with anxiety. I contemplated all the time it had taken for us to get to know each other better.

Even worse, I thought, what if I was being catfished? The term "catfish" is where a person meets another online using fake pictures and a false identity.

For all I knew, he could be a gigolo, a scam artist, or he could be married with children and mouths to feed back home. Look for the red flags, my research and friends warned. Check him out thoroughly. Did he work where he says he did on his profile? Better still, did everything seem to be truthful on his end?

We both had waited what seemed like forever for this moment. I had a lot of emotional baggage tied up in seeing this to the end. Still, I didn't want him to see me first, so I arrived in the parking area fifteen minutes early so I could turn around and back out of this meeting if I needed to.

To my massive relief, I recognized him immediately from his profile picture and other photos he'd posted on the online dating website.

"Read, take notes, click links, and google any questions you may have about this potential union," the sergeant from International Affairs told me as I explained my situation and plans. I'd taken a handful of brochures, pamphlets, and reports from his office to review thoroughly for my own sake.

"If all goes well, there are also other agencies that can help steer you through this process. Keep your head up. Think positive," I recalled his final words as I contemplated leaving without a trace.

From my initial glance from the car window, he looked much taller in person than I had imagined him to be.

We greeted each other slowly. I told him I would be wearing a business suit with a white leather belt. This is how we would recognize each other.

We both starred at one another without uttering a word. Silence. I had scanned him over and over a few times as I am sure he'd done likewise to me.

We both stood there motionless, gazing at one another.

I noticed his polished buffed dress shoes first. Reminiscent of the military-style shine of recruit boots, not a blemish in sight.

Absolute perfection. He wore faded jeans and a light blue sweater vest with a long-sleeved, freshly starched white shirt underneath.

We went in, found an open seat with a table, and sat next to each other. I followed my heart and knew it was leading me in the right direction.

The waiter peered at us and joked, "I see this is going well, should I bring out one plate or two?" pointing with his finger at our sitting so closely together a knife couldn't sever us apart.

Despite all these signs, I still had my doubts. He could turn out to be a lion in sheep's clothing, a stalker, or a kidnapper. I could read the newspaper headlines now, "Woman missing after meeting a stranger online for a date."

I wasn't ruling anything out. I've heard stranger stories in my day.

I reflected on my initial fears of signing on to an online international dating website. I never thought in all my born days that I would try meeting a suitor on the internet.

It started out as a dare from co-workers of mine to see if I would really do it or meet their challenge. After a long pause and quick breaths, I took the bait and signed on to an international dating website.

My hands were shaking, and you would think the person stood right in front of me in real-time. I made my profile and began my search.

I didn't have any particular preconceived notions about the experience other than my potential mate should be trustworthy, nice, smart, and someone I could entertain myself with on late nights after a couple of glasses of wine and a vivid fantasy. I settled on a few user profiles and began the journey.

I'd found a few websites that promised to make the experience a fulfilling one. There were actually several profiles that were an exact match to my personality and the things I'd mentioned I was looking for in a partner.

At the time, it had only been a few days since my profile went live, and it was already taking up the bulk of my time. It was all-consuming.

I thought that perhaps I was putting too much energy into this endeavor. Maybe I should take a few steps back and let it flow, I pondered.

Until one day, I got a special message. In the slew of them was this striking-looking man. I thought about the romance novels I used to read ravenously as a teen of a chance meeting between two people, they would fall in love and live happily ever after.

Yes, I was a hopeless romantic and still believed in falling in love at first sight. Corny, I know, but true.

Let me fill in a little bit more detail on how all this started and began to heat up.

You see, I am an American, and my fiancé is from Japan. We met on an international dating website. He often compared my experiences with his back in his country.

We fell in love and declared our undying love for one another. Quick, I know, but nevertheless, we knew it was right.

He proposed shortly after our initial encounter, and I now had 90 days to plan a wedding and get married to the man of my dreams. I felt compelled to do my homework in an area I knew nothing about.

Why only 90 days? Because the "fiancé visa," as we'll discuss later, only allows a 90-day stay unless you get married to your American citizen sponsor during that timeframe.

Yes, from meeting in person to marriage in 90 days or less.

This sounds like it could be the plot from a movie, but it could very well happen to you, especially since you're reading this book and are apparently interested in the prospect of international relationships.

Nowadays, dating might mean honing in some high-tech savvy. More and more hopeless romantics are expanding their search for love across international borders. The digital age opened the door to couples seeking a committed relationship filled with happiness and satisfaction.

This is what happened to me.

I'd just moved to Atlanta to finally complete my liberal arts degree and quickly began my search for a permanent job. I only knew a few people there, but at the behest of friends and family, I took the plunge and packed up all my belongings to lay my foundation in a new place.

The change was very necessary for me at that time. Things had become a real bore back home in Florida. Doing the same things repeatedly is enough to drive the sanest person crazy. I kept ending up with the same type of guy - that one guy who ended up just not being good for me at all.

When I met my match, that all changed. I took a leap of faith, and that leap paid off!

The digital age has spawned a wave of opportunities for those adventurous souls looking to test the waters of international dating.

Let's keep it real; meeting someone special and maintaining a healthy relationship is tough enough without adding distance to the mix. Yet, for countless hopeless romantics, technological advancements and the internet breathe a breath of fresh air into the dating world.

The social stigma surrounding meeting someone online is decreasing and more of the norm than the exception. Over half of Americans are familiar with a couple who met online, and attitudes are increasingly changing in a positive way.

There's a spike in people under 35 years of age as well as dating site users in their 40s, 50s, and 60s.

Those who may be challenged to meet a mate here in America can keep their options open, whether seeking something casual, a life partner, a serious relationship, or even marriage; overseas dating can offer something to tickle your fancy.

Legalities of International Relationships

In considering marrying a non-US citizen, make sure you follow the proper legal steps.

The technical name for the process of becoming a permanent America citizen is called naturalization.

If an American citizen wants to marry someone from another country, they would need to know details of that person's rights under US immigration laws.

While Americans have the freedom to marry the person of their choice provided it doesn't violate any laws. A person's immigration situation shouldn't have any bearing on if the marriage is recognized as legal.

This is a tedious process and will require some long hours and many forms and documents. The immigrant can be denied if he or she is noted inadmissible for having medical problems, a criminal background, or former immigration violations, or if authorities suspect the marriage is fraudulent only to obtain a green card.

Enlisting the assistance of an immigration attorney is a good alternative if the process becomes overwhelming and complicated. Don't take any chances. Mistakes in the application process could lead to denial or inadmissible application that could take years to correct.

These are some of the benefits of obtaining legal assistance:

- To find out if your spouse is eligible
- To find out your spouse's history or if there could be a problem of status on their part that would merit denial of the application for a green card
- Prepare immigration forms and other documents
- Establish the legitimacy of the relationship

- Attend immigration interview(s)

International marriage is a legal union between two partners from different countries. Nearly 40 to 50 percent of marriages in the United States end in divorce. Sixty percent of those people who remarry are likely to get divorced again.

As soon as your fiancé gets the visa approval, the two of you have up to 90 days to marry. It usually takes 6 months to a year to plan the usual American wedding, so your relationship will be on the fast track from the get-go. Of course, even while being long distance, your relationship will go through the same challenges (and rewards) as more traditional couples.

Marriage Fraud

All marriages for the purpose of gaining entry into the US as a permanent resident, federal Immigration laws deems fraudulent. Specifically, getting married only to obtain a green card leads to some serious consequences.

Marriage fraud is illegal and can lead to a penalty of up to $250,000 and spending years in prison. Often, US citizens are primary targets for marriage scams.

Make sure your fiancé is sincere with honest intentions beforehand. Check for the warning signs like:

- Your foreign national pushing you into quickly getting married
- Asking for money
- Concentrating on the benefits of his future US residency

Some international marriage laws require parental consent, affidavits, and proof of residency requirement to marry. Be sure to consult with your state's attorney general's office to ensure the international marriage is considered legal in the United States.

Fiancé Visa

The most common way a prospective mate enters the US to meet you is with a K-1 visa.

You can get the complete information and application procedures at the Department of State website at https://travel.state.gov/content/travel/en/us-visas/immigrate/family-immigration/nonimmigrant-visa-for-a-fiancé-k-1.html.

The process is relatively simple but is not without its limitations.

The first step in applying for a fiancé visa is for the US citizen counterpart to file a "Petition for Alien Fiancé" that can be found at the US Citizenship and Immigration Services website https://www.uscis.gov/i-129f.

Second, the foreign national fiancé should apply for a K-1 visa.

Dependant children of the foreign boyfriend/girlfriend can also apply for their own K visa, called a K-2. This allows the child to travel to the US along with their parent, or they may "follow-to-join" within one year.

Next, the foreign national must collect the required documents and prepare for an interview. These documents (and special procedures) include:

- Proof of a completed DS-160 online visa application
- A valid passport
- Birth certificate
- If previously married, they must supply either a divorce or death certificate for both themselves and the US citizen sponsor.
- Police certificates

- Medical examination along with vaccinations
- Evidence of financial support, which may include Form I-134 (https://www.uscis.gov/i-134)
- 2 photographs – with the same qualities as a passport photo
    - 2x2 size
    - In color
    - Taken within the past 6 months
    - Cannot wear a hat, glasses, headphones, jewelry
- Evidence of your relationship with the US sponsor
- Payment of fees

Some evidence of financial support from the US sponsor may include such documentation as:

- A copy of your last federal income tax
- A signed statement from your employer
- A signed statement from an officer of your bank with account information

Don't be shy about sharing very personal information. The government is very thorough in this regard. To prove that my long-distance boyfriend and I were a couple, he had to provide phone records and text message logs to prove that we spoke often.

We were an unusual case in that we had not met at all in person until he traveled to the United States via this K-1 visa. Usually, you have to have met at some point within the past two years before you can even apply for a K-1 visa. I never had the money to travel to meet him.

Immigration Support

You can also get immigration support for visas and resident statuses in order to start the citizenship journey in the following ways:

- Have the foreign spouse-to-be take English language learning and citizenship classes from the US Citizenship and Immigration Services agency or other referrals that assist immigrants.
- Consider getting legal support to navigate any struggles with visas or resident status. The ARAG legal insurance plan (https://www.araglegal.com/) offers members access to attorneys for legal advice and consultations on the immigration process, guidelines, petitions, laws, deportation regulations, immigrant benefits, regulations and deportation proceedings. They may also help with applications and any immigration hearings.

There is a listing of some renown immigration attorneys in the appendix at the end of this book. If nothing else, they may be able to provide you with a free consultation or give you direction to find a good attorney that is more local to you.

After the Wedding

A K-1 visa is issued with the specific conclusion in mind that the foreign national intends to marry their citizen sponsor.

This must be completed within the 90-day timeframe or they risk deportation and sanctions against any further application for entry into the United States.

Once you are legally and truly married, the immigrant spouse may apply for a green card. According to the Department of Homeland Security's website (https://www.uscis.gov/greencard/fiancées),

> *"After being admitted to the United States as a K-1 nonimmigrant and marrying the US citizen petitioner within 90 days, the alien spouse can then apply for lawful permanent resident status in the United States (get a Green Card)."*

The act of marriage qualifies the spouse who is visiting on a K-1 visa to apply for an "adjustment of status." This status adjustment allows the spouse to expedite jumping through some legal hoops, so to speak.

The lengthy process of obtaining a status adjustment is outlined as the following conditions:

- You properly file Form I-485 (https://www.uscis.gov/i-485supa), Application to Register Permanent Residence or Adjust Status
- You are physically present in the United States at the time you file your Form I-485
- You were inspected and admitted to the United States on a K-1 nonimmigrant visa
- Within 90 days of being admitted into the United States as a K-1 nonimmigrant, you entered into a bona fide marriage with the US citizen who filed Form I-129F, Petition for Alien Fiancé(e) for you (which you have to do in order to get a K-1 visa anyway)
- None of the applicable bars to adjustment of status apply to you.
- You are admissible to the United States for lawful permanent residence.

Note that an immigrant visa is always available to you if you marry your US citizen petitioner within 90 days of being admitted as a K-1 nonimmigrant. Once you marry, you are treated as an immediate relative.

Some of the "bars to adjustment" might include any act that you made that violated immigration law. The good news is that once the marriage happens, the foreign national is considered to be an immediate relative. This brings with it some excused conditions that might have otherwise resulted in denying the adjustment of status.

These bars of adjustment that no longer hinder an immigrant spouse might include if they ever worked or are working illegally or if they ever failed to maintain lawful status since entry into the United States continuously. These conditions, once being made a relative, will no longer keep the spouse from gaining an adjustment of immigration status.

The road to successful immigration is tough. Gaining the support of a good immigration lawyer would be my advice.

Precautions to Take

Many singles would love to date someone of a different race or country but simply don't know how. Do your homework before you take the leap.

Apparently, there's some truth to the adage that "distance makes the heart grow fonder," at least for those looking for their prince/princess charming.

It's imperative to discuss this issue at the beginning of our exploration through the crevices of the international dating world. While not all online connections are made with ill-intentions, there is, however, a slew of people who are legitimately and honestly eager to make a relationship connection.

Some critics, being the skeptics that they are, would cry that all online dating interactions are bad and dangerous. Potential online dating users should always exercise caution.

When in doubt, don't share personal information like your address, phone number, or other personal information that could potentially place you in danger or put you in harm's way. By no means should you share your bank account information, credit card numbers, or your social security number with anyone.

Your foreign fiancé or love interest may want to desperately flee their country and cross US borders by any means necessary. Unfortunately, there are people who seek to prey on innocent women and men for money or the monetary benefits that it could bring.

Monitor the actions of the person on the other end of the computer screen.

Marriage green card scams, con-artists, and dating site fraud are at the top of the list in domestic and overseas online dating.

As an American and a woman, I've learned a thing or two about what to do and definitely what not to do when visiting online dating websites and other registered users from overseas. My knowledge is based on these experiences and will hopefully help you make your next dating (long-distance or otherwise) relationship better.

Green card and dating site fraud rise to the top of the list of concerns involving international online dating. The reasons vary in terms of American citizens and foreign nationals.

I would warn, and the experts agree, against being targeted by a foreign national who professes an instant love interest in you.

Obtaining a green card can be so desired that someone may use your heart as a means to an end for gaining into the United States. Many times, after the foreign national gets the card, they will leave the US citizen or make life difficult and the citizen will abandon him or her.

A foreign national could con the US citizen out of money via wiring money overseas. Unfortunately, the internet doesn't always provide the needed protection against fraud. Most times, the transaction is anonymous and may not offer the correct details like the recipient's name, age, nationality, or marital status.

Romance scams may cost tens of thousands of dollars by way of sending money to another party. You may be pressured to pay for travel expenses for the foreign national to come to the United States or for you to go to his country of origin.

You may be asked to fork over the cost of an immigration attorney or the filing fees for visas and passports and the like. Often, the US sponsor is stuck taking care of the scammer once they arrive in the United States by providing clothing, shelter, and gifts.

Many victims of the scam have damaged their credit by taking out loans or lines of credit to assist the scammer.

Qualities That Should Raise Suspicion

Ways to spot a dating site fraud from a foreign national:

- Hasty professions of love, desire, or sex.
- Asking for money right away.
- Restrictions on how you can contact or talk to them.

- The person quickly tries to move the relationship from a monitored site to a personal email account.
- Sending money for visas or travel tickets and the foreign national never seems to make it.

Ways you can protect yourself include:

- Ask to verify the authenticity of the profile picture or photographs that look like they were taken at a studio.
- Learn everything you an about obtaining a visa, green cards, and website dating fraud.
- Have a detailed conversation with the potential suitor. Hopefully, if you are really serious about pursuing marriage with them, you should have many hours of conversations with them!
- Never send money for any reason or contact the State's Department of Fraud Prevention Unit at FPMM@state.gov.
- Be sure to report suspected dating site scams or fraud immediately to the Federal Bureau of Investigation's Internet Crime Complaint Center
- Report the profile of the fraud perpetrator on the dating site.
- **Do your homework to find out as much as you can about the foreign national like a picture on their visa.**

There's Still Hope!

On the flip side, there are people making honest, loving, and caring connections every day with the help of international dating websites.

Each day, I would look forward to my boyfriend's love music playing on my voicemail, professing his undying commitment to me and only me.

Had all this been a hoax to see if he could pull it off successfully without anyone being the wiser? I kept my wits about me, but I wasn't giving up on him so quickly.

If nothing else, I was at least going to give our relationship a fighting chance even if it included crossing overseas borders.

Another demographic that is usually stereotyped as an antisocial loner is the video game player. You know – that archetype of the single, overweight guy who at age 30 still lives in his parent's basement and plays video games all day? That's the look.

Well, to my surprise, this stereotype doesn't really hold up. Most adults who consider themselves to be serious online gamers hold steady jobs, support themselves, and are looking for relationships, too. They are more open to the idea of meeting their soulmate online.

Even with the exhaustive research I'd conducted, I was even surprised to learn that the single gamer was less common than you might think. This demographic had been a previously unexplored area in the dating world.

This is what I learned about international dating websites for gamers. There is a new spin of websites cropping up in the online dating scene, and that is international dating for gamers.

There are an estimated 2.2 billion gamers in the world of the entire 7.6 billion people on the earth. Of the 2.2 billion gamers, 1.2 billion play those games on a PC.

The growing number of recreational gamers spurred interest in establishing a platform for singles to meet other singles with similar interests. For example, facebook.com/dating boasts that it allows users to create an independent profile showing interest in another profiler.

The platform lets users contact each other. They can then match with other people of common interests. The business is adding a "Secret Crush" and like components. Facebook Dating uses filters such as location, number of children, religion, age, and height to search for a match on its platform.

With so many people successfully finding love online, it's worth giving it a shot, despite the precautions.

A Match Made in Heaven

Marriage Brokers

You may want to consider using the services of an international marriage broker. An international marriage broker (IMB) could be a corporation, partnership, business, individual, or established legal entity whose sole purpose is to provide dating, matrimonial, or dating matchmaking services between US citizens and foreign nationals.

An international marriage broker is a company that charges a fee for providing matchmaking services between US citizens or permanent residents and foreign nationals

IMBs are viewed as an add-on to the $2 billion dating industry. There are an estimated 600 IMBs currently in operation.

This trade started in South East Asia and soon expanded to Latin America and the former Soviet Union, particularly the Ukraine. The practice dates back all the way to 1998.

The US Immigration and Naturalization department reports there are 10,000 marriages annually initiated by IMBs.

The International Marriage Brokers Regulation Act of 2005 (IMBRA) is a United States federal statute that stipulates a background check for marriage visa sponsors and limits serial visa applications.

The law also requires background checks for United States citizens enlisting the service of a marriage broker. This is particularly for dating services involving US citizens and foreign nationals at a cost.

A legal precedent was set in the Susanna Blackwell case from 1995 and the Anastasia King case of 2000, where foreign women were being abused by men using the K-1 fiancé visa approved by the US State Department to sponsor them to the United States.

The King case involved the husband physically abusing a former bride and murdering Anastasia. The two had met through a Moscow advertisement.

The IMBRA is intended to ensure the safety of women clients. Provisions of the IMBRA include:

- The prohibition of marketing of anyone under the age of 18.
- The IMB agency must require a background check of US clients to share with foreign nationals in the foreigner's native language.
- The disclosure of US citizens of any crimes committed before completing a form 1-129F Petition for Alien Fiancé.
- Places limitations on the number of times a US citizen can petition a foreign fiancé.

Check the Legitimacy of an Agency

The International Association of the Better Business Bureaus (IABBB), located in Mexico, Canada, and the United States, is a great resource to find out if the international dating entity is legit. The IABBB is a network of interconnected businesses registered in these locations mentioned above. (https://www.bbb.org/local-bbb/international-association-of-better-business-bureaus)

This agency is committed to encouraging honest relations between businesses and consumers. This supports consumer confidence and a trustworthy environment for everyone involved.

You can contact them if needed at:

3033 Wilson Blvd, Arlington, VA 22201, Phone: 703-276-0100.

These are some registered users of the International Better Business Bureau listed in the appendix at the end of this book.

International Matchmaking Services

International matchmaking services add a new twist to finding love.

At some point, you may come to the realization that you may not meet the love of your life on a dating app.

According to Cox at the Better Business Bureau, hiring a matchmaking service costs a minimum of $5,000 and some as high as $10.000. But if you are serious about a soulmate, a matchmaker could be the answer to your prayers.

This would make a lot a sense because you could detail what you are looking for in a person and have the professional look around to find a good fit. A few top-of-the-line international matchmaker agencies and services are listed in the appendix at the end of this book.

One last note, in choosing to go with one of these listed services, you get the assurance that the professional will do everything to search for the perfect suitor for you.

Navigating the International Singles World

I'll explain how all of this started between myself and international singles, which led to my meeting my husband.

My Story

I knew a girl named Candy that I went to high school with. Around the schoolyard, she always hung out with the popular crowd, always had groupies who followed behind her everywhere she went and followed her about to everything she did. Completely my opposite or so I thought.

Candy was well-traveled, accustomed to meeting different types of people from around the world from the stories she would tell me. Her father was a diplomat and entertained across the globe.

She'd grown accustomed to this type of environment of meeting men online. I had only remained in the same neighborhood in the same city for as long as I could remember around the same thing and the same type of people. Reading and submerging myself with cheap paperback novels to occupy my time and quenched the boredom festering inside of me.

Candy and I kept in touch, even after she moved away just before our senior year. When I graduated high school, I yearned to get out of my hometown in Florida. I moved to

Atlanta, took a job as an office clerk, and took classes at Georgia State.

(Fun fact - Julia Roberts, the famous actress, went to Georgia State University!)

My days were becoming mundane. I wasn't finding a niche of friends at school, and many of my coworkers were much older than me, most married with children. They weren't keen on going out on Fridays after work for a drink.

I was lamenting to a coworker one day that I had no luck with guys. I was feeling the need to start looking towards my very serious future. Would I ever settle down and become a mom?

The coworkers then dared me to sign up on a dating site, but not just any dating site. They encouraged me, rather strongly and jokingly, to enlist on an international dating website. The rest of the story was governed by fate!

One of the first people I thought to call about my engagement was my friend Candy. She was super happy for me, but she still warned me to be on the lookout for scammers and websites promising one thing for a hefty fee when it turns out to be quite another.

From her worldly travels, she had heard too many stories about men who sought to prey upon the heartstrings of lonely American women – especially, as she said, "Those who are as cute as you are, my dear!" I smiled when she said that. She always had a way to make me feel better.

Candy also emphasized to be careful of the men who messaged you if you feel they didn't have good intentions and just wanted to search the lot of available, desperate, lonely women.

Even with everyone's kind words of caution, I still felt my heart pulling me in the direction of meeting my life partner in this more unconventional way. The men in my life were just not measuring up the way I had hoped, even after moving to a new city.

I set my sights, and my heart, on meeting my other half online – even if he lived in a totally different country!

My Advice

Online dating websites or apps are a great starting place to find your prince charming. With just a click of the mouse, you could easily develop a list of approachable suiters.

Don't spend countless hours weeding through unsuitable men when you can find your romantic match with just a swipe of a finger.

Be aware that everyone doesn't speak English. English comes in third place as the most spoken language in the world. Don't assume your date from another country knows how to speak English. If most of your initial conversation is via typing, texting, or other written messaging, he may be using a translator program to converse with you.

Study the language and culture of your foreign date as well as teach him yours. This is a great activity to see first-hand how you both interact together.

You don't have to put everything on the table just yet on your profile, but try at best to be as honest as possible. Don't fabricate the truth.

Do not lie on your profile. Avoid this temptation in attempting to put your best foot forward. If you're lucky and the meeting blossoms into something more long-term and serious, you've started a relationship with your foreign date based on lies. This means being as honest as possible about your age, height, and weight.

Stay away from cliché pickup lines. They are called pick up lines for a reason and are meant for those not looking to stick around long. Any communication barriers and slang terms may mean something totally different to the other person.

Don't talk about the exes to one another. This doesn't leave a good impression and is unfair to the other party you're in front of now. It may give off the vibe that you're still into your former lover or haven't moved on from the former relationship.

I remembered how I was flattered that my fiancé had taken the time to read my entire profile and decided to get the nerve to reach out to me.

He didn't appear to have any preconceived notions or expectations on the matter for companionship someone to spend quality time with.

I am sure my story is atypical in terms of the world of online dating and far from the norm for anybody lucky enough to meet the love of their life, get engaged, and then start planning a wedding in less than 90 days.

Challenges of Long-Distance Courtship

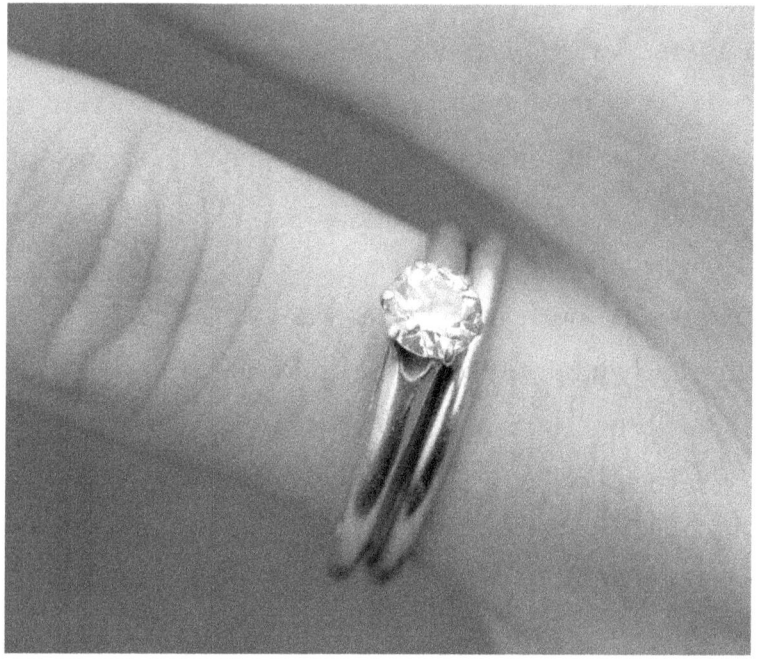

There are distinct challenges for an international couple.

First, what is the definition of an international couple? Basically, each person in the relationship comes from different counties and cultures.

These may be people who:

- Teachers who live and work abroad
- A couple from different cultures who may live in a third country
- A relationship where one partner travels abroad extensively
- Married students who study abroad

Every relationship may need a little help every now and again. International couples require a great deal of effort and emotion from either party.

I have assembled a list of resources in the appendix that can offer some relief to couples, whether it is to seek advice, discuss a troubling issue, or find ways to cope with the distance and loneliness.

These resources may also give advice as to the best ways to successfully get the spouse-to-be into the United States legally.

Take your time and participate in the forums and message boards. If nothing else, you have made a connection with others who are or were once in your situation.

Overcoming Rumors and Prejudice

I'll be honest, the overshadowing of rumors that my international fiancé only asked me to marry him to enter the United States as a permanent citizen, dulled the spark between us just a little.

Admittedly, our relationship heated up quickly. I sometimes felt like I was the one pushing him more into the relationship by usually being the first to message him or to initiate a Skype call.

In reality, the time difference was so that basically, my boyfriend was about 14 hours ahead of me! My early morning was his late-night and vice-versa. We also both had full-time jobs, so our respective daytime hours were usually spent working.

I cherished weekends all the more because it meant that we stayed up late for each other, talking constantly. Sometimes, I would just put my phone on a Facetime call and just have him with me while I did mundane stuff like grocery shopping and household chores. I was just so happy to have him share my day-to-day life with me, even if he "lived" in my phone!

Hon came from a well-to-do family in Tokyo. His father descended from a long lineage of surgeons, and his mom was a renowned microbiologist. Despite all his social stature, he would be viewed as an outsider for desiring to gain full US citizenship through marriage.

Worse yet, America could very well not be as he had imagined. I learned quickly that although America is more sophisticated and worldly since its Japanese history during WWII, some do not forgive and forget. Hatred can sometimes run deep and is repeated for generations.

Mixed-race couples could face prejudice and discrimination on both sides of the long-held hatred and fear against inter-race relationships here in the states and abroad.

Decades ago, when the Japanese attacked Pearl Harbor in 1941, killing 2,400 Americans, the United States countered the assault and ultimately dropped two atomic bombs on Japan. Japan ultimately surrendered to American allies, which ended the war.

Some people would treat my husband-to-be differently based on his ethnicity. It would be viewed as sleeping with the enemy. This is one consideration that I was willing to work with him on combatting.

My family had moved up the social ladder through owning a rural sugar farm and the money that came with it. I was one of the few family members to seek a life away from those humble beginnings.

I'd achieved my level of success and accomplishment without their power or influence. The flip side of this is the impact of going it on my own without their safety net to catch me.

I became somewhat ostracized as it was viewed that I was turning my back on my family because I didn't want to travel down the same road as they had done for generations. In the same way, Hon was also choosing this sort of path.

This created a wedge, a soft-spot between my family and myself. I wasn't turning my back on the elders who had worked tirelessly to build a strong foundation for me to survive the harsh realities of the world.

I simply couldn't continue to live that pretentious lifestyle any longer of the haves-and-the-have-nots or carry the weight of my elders who'd pathed that tortuous path for me to stand on. I could make it on my own no matter what this would bring- even the perils of an international wedding.

Decisions to Make

Besides the stress of getting married and spending the rest of my life with my fiancé, I was overwhelmed with putting things into perspective.

First on the list were a few non-negotiable items that needed to be taken care of at the outset. I actually wrote a physical list of decisions we needed to make. I felt like there were important factors to discuss to ensure we were on the same page.

In addition, I suggested that we should seek premarital counseling online to make this transition to married life a smooth one. While participating in these sessions, several decisions that had been up in the air were resolved.

Here are some of them and their outcome:

Prenuptial agreements. We mutually agreed that a prenuptial agreement would be in both of our best interests, considering the unorthodox nature of our relationship. We both agreed that we each would keep whatever net worth we came into the marriage with and only share monies and other valuables like the house and other items that were acquired while we were together. We also enlisted the assistance of a family law attorney who would work in collaboration with lawyers in his country should the need arise.

Where to have the wedding ceremony. I tried to be as fair as possible about this issue. My fiancé wanted to please me, so we agreed to have the wedding in the US, and the reception abroad in his country.

This mutual compromise was a benefit to everyone involved. This would allow both families to be involved and share in our big day in some way.

Traditions. We decided to respectfully keep fundamental traditions from both cultures and simply merge them into one whole. Along with my wedding coordinator, my maid -of - honor promised to oversee these transitions and turned them into a beautiful ensemble.

Each family could add in these ideas, customs, and traditions in the end. Marriage was a give and take. Compromise for either party makes for a happy future life together.

I will discuss much more about the actual wedding planning in a following chapter.

Religion. We took to a traditional Christian faith-walk because he respectfully knew I wouldn't have it any other way. Fortunately, he was an avid practicing Christian in his native country while respecting his elder's differing views. "Agree to disagree," the counselor had stated as one of the first rules of thumb for making a successful marriage.

Understanding the other's opinions and perspectives on fundamental matters are crucial to a long, happy life together.

Children. This was an important issue for both of us. Even though neither of us was thinking of making a "honeymoon baby," we both knew we eventually did want to start a family together.

We mutually decided that we would raise the children in America, and they would have summer visits with his side of the family. This way, the children could get the benefit of a dual culture.

Culture. During counseling, my fiancé discussed how important it would be to him for the children to learn to speak and read Japanese. This way, they would have an important part of his heritage, and they could more easily speak with their relatives on his side.

I agreed that this was the best of both worlds, so to speak, for our future family. Being bilingual would be an amazing advantage for our children.

Family and friends. All friends and relatives are required to be trustworthy and respectful to each one of us on either side. If not, they were barred from association equally.

This may seem harsh, but we valued the support of our friends and family. If they could not get behind us in this matter, then they could get away from us. It was a healthy boundary for us to draw, to be honest.

Finances. Ensure that you can afford to live and visit abroad. We also had to decide when and where and what sort of vocation Hon would have when he finally was legally allowed to work in America. We agreed that it might mean that he was a "house husband" for a little while as he would try to become established. He actually did not relish the idea of being dependant upon his future wife financially and vowed to become a provider as soon as he could.

Finances are sometimes an uncomfortable subject, but it is very much one that needs to be addressed beforehand. Couples should decide who will work, where you will live, and what your financial quality of life will be like. It would be unfair for an international spouse to expect to live in a mansion if you think the two of you will, in reality, live in a tiny studio apartment. These choices should be discussed.

My living in America would make frequent trips to his country a necessity. This is not the perfect plan by any means but was discussed and agreed upon well before we became engaged.

Talking and making final agreements create a happy relationship. If you are truly in love and committed, you both will find a way to make it work.

Compromise is the name of the game.

Planning the Big Day!

Suggestions from family and friends to have two weddings - one in America and the other in my fiancé's country seemed a bit over-the-top as well as expensive.

We both finally decided to have the wedding in the US and plan a reception in his hometown. Planning a celebration in another country was exciting but tiresome.

Language barriers and cultural customs almost short-cut the entire plan. The rather short engagement period didn't really give the invited extended family and friends time to save up the money to make the trip to visit us. Really, none of his immediate family could attend the wedding.

While in America, my fiancé decided that he wanted a bachelor party. He didn't really know anyone here, so I enlisted some male coworkers to show him a good time. They good-naturedly took him out to a sports bar and showed him how to shout at a football game.

When thinking about the enormous details of my wedding day, I was overcome with feeling like it was just too much to deal with. I really just wanted to be married to Hon, but I also wanted it to be an experience that I could remember fondly.

I consulted with family and friends who were already married, and they came up with these wedding models as the best choice for an international bride and groom. I also made the decision to hire a wedding planner. I just felt like that money would be well-spent in ensuring that my big day getting hitched went off without a hitch (pun intended, of course)!

I have included a list of some of the top wedding planners from my home state of Florida. We had decided to hold the ceremony there, as that was where my family mostly was, and I knew of a lovely little beachside chapel where we could hold the ceremony.

Make Lists!

Making lists are the only way I know to stay sane. If I don't write something down, I tend to forget it quickly.

Here is my list of practical advice to you:

- Make a list of the issues to keep in mind when planning the details of the event with your partner.
- Keep expenses small by inviting a small guest list. May be forced to decrease the guest list and make it for a smaller essential group.
- Too expensive for my family to travel outside of the United States to attend the wedding.
- It allows my future husband's family a chance to get acquainted with my culture when they visit us in the US.
- Write down the advantages and disadvantages of the collective plan.
- The wedding is all about my friends and me on my big day.
- My family wouldn't get to know my fiancé's family members initially.

The budget for our wedding was the biggest deciding factor in the choices that had to be made. There were a host of things to consider.

Foremost, is the protruding question, "Is he worth all this effort?" and I most certainly felt that, yes, he was. That first meeting in person at that chain restaurant cemented the deal, at least for me.

Blending Traditions

At the end of the day, where to hold the wedding was a no-brainer, really. We agreed it would be best to be in America because of the expense of the traditional obligation required in Japan.

Also, since he was coming to me on a K-1 visa, we only had 90 days to see the wedding through. It just made sense to plan and hold it in America.

While only a small percentage of Japanse citizens are Christians, I was fortunate that my fiancé shared my religious beliefs. He was totally on board with being married by an ordained pastor in a chapel and reciting Biblical text during the ceremony.

While the ceremony was mostly composed of traditional Christian-American elements, we did, however, decide to incorporate many Japanese traditions and culture in the American wedding, such as including 500 origami cranes in the decorations.

This also included a cherry blossom centerpiece at each guest table for our little cocktail hour. The cherry blossom was also printed on all the party favors and wedding invitations.

I would wear a traditional western culture white dress with a matching vale. My maid of honor older sister would wear a beige and cherry blossom pink dress. My husband chose to wear a traditional Japanese wedding suit.

Pushing the Budget

Of course, these accommodations could have pushed the wedding budget over the original plan, but my wedding planner was diligent in finding all the deals she could muster. She was well worth her fee!

We both agreed to keep the total cost of the entire ceremony under $5,000, which would mean nearly emptying my savings and pushing the limit on money borrowed from family.

I was lucky enough to find a wedding coordinator with skills who could work with my limited budget. She scaled down the total cost of the wedding at a real discount without jeopardizing quality for $4,500.

Whatever areas where she could cut corners, she did. Saving money was the priority. Still, the main thing I got from this were the benefits of having someone experienced by my side to work with vendors, to ask important questions that I may have forgotten to ask, to stay on top of issues like contracts, paperwork, contact information, schedules, and a day-to-day timeline of even the smallest details and deadlines.

I found my wedding coordinator by word of mouth through a co-worker whose sister was getting married before me. I contracted with her for a real steal of $1,000, compared to other high-end coordinators in my local area.

Search message boards and https://www.thumbtack.com/ to find wedding coordinators off the traditional radar with proven talent at reasonable prices. It may take some effort on your part, but it will be well worth the digging in the end.

This is the final detailed budget. There would be a total of 50 guests in attendance.

Venue: $100 reservation fee

Pastor's fee for his time: $100, although this man was a family friend, and we did not have the requirement of completing premarital counseling with him in order for him to marry us

Groom's Attire: $200

Here's a big one – My dress: $0, because my mother purchased it! It actually would have cost us well over $200.

Catering of appetizers, servers, cleaners, and other hospitality: $1,000

Alcohol and drinks: $375, for one drink per person, otherwise it was a cash bar. The upside is that we only hosted a cocktail hour while we took pictures, and not a full reception- initially anyway.

Email and designed invitations: $25 for postage. We really only had to mail invites to about 20 people, so I designed them myself and printed them myself. Others were invited via email or even word of mouth and didn't require a paper invite.

Music: $0, we used an iPod with a Bluetooth speaker! Fancy, I know!

Decorations: $500. Origami paper is no joke!

Makeup and hair donated by a friend: $0

Other miscellaneous expenses: $200

Photographer: $1,000

Wedding coordinator's fee: $1,000. That was well worth it!

That's a grand total of $4,500, just for the ceremony and a small cocktail hour reception of sorts. This didn't even include the reception we wanted to have in Japan.

As of the time I am writing this book, we have yet to plan that reception for Hon's family. I really cannot wait to really get to know my new in-laws. We have talked often on the phone and Facetime, with Hon translating, and they are super supportive of us! I am relieved that they have accepted me into the Sato family.

Overseas LGBT Couples

LGBTQ is the acronym for lesbian, gay, bisexual, transgender, queer, and questioning. This growing community is growing quickly and becoming more nuanced every day.

My new brother-in-law is also from Japan, and he is openly homosexual. I am extremely excited to meet him in person someday soon!

He asked me to lend any assistance I could provide in obtaining a visa or green card for one of his close friends so he can marry his long-time same-sex partner, who is an American.

I feared that this could turn into a very complicated, time-consuming feat on my end. I had to meet with the same immigration attorney for help and a clearer understanding of the procedures.

I thought it strange that my fiancé hardly ever mentioned his brother while we were courting. I don't think he was ashamed of him, but honestly, I think it was such a nonchalant thing for him that he didn't think it was a particular point of interest.

The Legalities

In doing my research, this is what I found:

The biggest immigration-related ruling occurred with the 2013 Supreme Court Windsor decision, where the high court overturned portions of the federal Defense of Marriage Act (DOMA) to now allow US residents to petition for green cards for their same-sex spouses. Previously, DOMA's definition of marriage as a union between a man and a woman.

US citizens are allowed to apply for a fiancé visa to marry a same-sex partner in the United States. The 2015 Supreme Court decision allowed same-sex marriages legal in all 50 states.

Only 13% of the member countries in the United Nations condone gay marriages, and of that number, a mere 5% have a law written into their constitutions, making it illegal to discriminate based on sexual orientation.

China's government recently announced that it would not expand marriage to include same-sex partners. This comes on the heels of Taiwan which became a pioneer in becoming the first country in Asia to legalize same-sex marriage.

Even with the legalization of same-sex marriages in the United States, 35% of other countries in the United Nations make it illegal to do so.

Even more horrifying is same-sex acts continue to carry the death penalty in some countries who practice Islamic sharia law like Iran, Saudi Arabia, Yemen, Nigeria, Sudan, and Somalia where same-sex of any kind is a capital offense. The majority of Muslim nations outlaw homosexuality in the Middle East, Southeast Asia, and Africa.

LGBT Dating Sites

Regardless of how you identify - gay, straight, or otherwise - more than likely, there is an online dating platform that has a domestic or global reach to suit your liking.

I feel compelled to state that gay women and men represent a diverse, unique group of people with different views, preferences, and various demographics joined by gender identity and sexual orientation.

Up until recently, dating websites were geared almost exclusively on the whims of only straight people. Today, developers are catering to an additional niche audience: the single lesbian woman and the single gay man.

But these days, dating apps are not only created with a focus on straight people. Members of the LGBT community are quick to decry apps and websites whose claim to embrace every user only to indirectly ostracize the queer males and lesbian women looking for love, friendship, companionship, marriage, or a hookup online with its cookie-cutter approach.

There is a need to go well-beyond standard matches but rather filters or barriers to entry. Connection matches have to go deeper to include personality, background, and other compatibility criteria.

Members of the LGBT community are as much deserving of love and affection as the next person. The challenges they oftentimes face as a same-sex-single is finding someone who piques their interests, finding meaningful connections, and knowing which websites offer the best options.

Gay bars are quickly becoming a thing of the past and are a dying breed of places to meet other singles.

The standard netiquette still applies to online users of all demographics despite their sexual orientation and requires that all users list themselves as whatever they choose to say or identify as similar to revealing if you are a drinker or a smoker.

In the appendix, I've compiled a list of user-friendly websites and apps for LGBT daters.

The Tinders and the Bumbles are mainstream dating apps that started out with the target audience of straight people, yet has since gained strides in being an invaluable resource for the LGBT community.

Safety Concerns

Needless-to-say, daters, in general, are exercising caution and a safety-first technique as it applies to online dating, domestically and internationally.

Beware of posting your real full name, address, and any financial information in too many places. Never send money to anyone who you have never met in real life.

Do not agree to go on a first date with someone at their house or apartment.

Most dating websites and apps allow users to report suspicious behavior, harassment, bullying, and creeping.

It is unfortunate that a great deal of LGBTQ singles can become targets of abuse on dating websites. There was a recent survey that found 35% of gay men were reportedly harassed by someone online. There were 65% who felt satisfied with their experience.

LBGT community members who want to connect with other singles of the same-sex is a clear case of buyer beware. Even on straight-centered websites, users should exercise some level of caution for spammers and scammers.

Sometimes people feel that they are falling in love an instead are falling for a lie. Use your best judgment in avoiding fake websites and con-artists.

For example, beware of profiles that do not use pictures and don't utilize the website's authentication tools in building trust with other similar singles. Zoosk has this option where the developers have a photo verification system to prove they are who they say they are.

Don't Give Up!

Still, LGBTQ singles can rest easy when meeting someone online; there are some people who are kind, sincere, and worthy of getting to know better. This simply takes a little practice, and before you know it, you will operate like a pro.

Hopefully, the LGBTQ websites will offer promising encounters and engagements whether you are gay, bisexual, or lesbian in finding interested singles.

Barriers

Another critical component of the LGBTQ community is same-sex marriage. This the legal union between two people of the same sex and gender who have entered into a civil or religious ceremony.

Same-sex marriages stem all the way back to the first century. In modern times, same-sex marriages began to be legalized in the 21st century and are available in 28 countries. These are the countries and jurisdictions where same-sex marriages are recognized:

Argentine	Australia	Austria
Belgium	Brazil	Canada
Columbia	Denmark	Ecuador
Finland	France	Germany
Iceland	Ireland	Luxembourg
Malta	Mexico	The Netherlands
New Zealand	Norway	Portugal
South Africa	Spain	Sweden
Taiwan	The United Kingdom	The United States
Uruguay		

Countries like Costa Rica, Armenia, Bulgaria are set to rule on the issue of same-sex couple's overseas marriages soon.

Same-sex marriage is recognized in some jurisdictions deriving from changes in marriage laws, court rulings, and the constitutional rights of equity guaranteed by law.

Some advocates feel strongly in support of same-sex marriages because they feel it is a basic human and civil right. Conversely, the opposition to same-sex marriages comes mostly from religious fundamentalist organizations.

If your home state refuses to marry you and your same-sex spouse, I recommend that you try another state or country to get married.

These are some important essentials to consider in making this decision:

- Ask yourself and your partner if you truly want to build your lives together financially?
- Does the home state or country offer any protections to same-sex couples?
- Where will you live after marriage? Is it a hostile or non-hostile environment?

- If you or your spouse-to-be is receiving public assistance, the marriage could jeopardize your eligibility and cause you to lose some or all of your benefits.
- How will the new couple fill out their tax returns?
- Will you or your spouse qualify for health and other employer-sponsored spousal benefits?

While you can sue if you feel you have been discriminated against because of the same-sex marriage issue, these actions are lengthy and costly.

Investigate what your state or country protections are for civil unions, domestic partnerships, and who the designated person is with authority to make medical and other important decisions if you are unable to. Find out the requirements to get married in your state or country.

If a state domestic partnership doesn't exist, contact your state or local LGBT group or legislator(s). I have included an appendix listing of some of the most prominent LGBT advocacy groups for your reference.

Most LGBTQ couples are married in a state or foreign country that honors same-sex marriages. When couples already reside in these areas, it makes for a non-hostile, friendly place as well as others to travel there for marriage.

Victories

In a precedential case, the Supreme Court ruled that the Section of DOMA (Defense of Marriage Act) as a union between a man and a woman violates the Equal Protection Clause and is therefore unconstitutional.

Previously, jurisdictions had limited benefits to opposite-sex married couples, not recognizing the authenticity of same-sex married couples. What we know now is federal agencies like the Social Security Administration look to the residence of the couple and the spouse's employment history in order to determine whether same-sex married couples are entitled to benefits.

On the other hand, federal agencies like the Citizenship and Immigration Services (USCIS) look at the location where the celebration occurred or where the marriage was performed for same-sex couples to determine eligible awards.

Notwithstanding, the US Department of Treasury ruled that same-sex marriages where couples were married in the United

States, the District of Columbia, or other US jurisdiction or foreign country, is recognized and considered married in terms of all federal tax provisions when marriage is an issue. This rule does not legally hold up with same-sex couples in domestic or civil partnerships.

I didn't take any chances and consulted with an attorney regarding our immigration matters. I would suggest for you to also check with an attorney who specializes in these dealings.

Advice for the Older Single

Seniors looking for love, companionship, or a serious relationship can do so right from the comfort of their own homes, thanks to the growing number of niche dating websites with this audience in mind.

Senior dating websites are increasing day by day, along with the growth of a more mature population.

This is the case for both domestic and international daters.

A recent survey found that from 2013 to 2016, there was an increase in the number of seniors tapping into the online dating world. In fact, the amount doubled from 6% to 12%.

Seniors are looking online to quench loneliness and to have someone to share experiences with, like watching a movie, going to the park, hanging out with, and even marrying.

Older people tend to have different motivations for participating in online dating websites than the younger generations.

As an older person looking for love or companionship, there is no need to fear this opportunity. Mostly, senior dating sites are exclusively tailored for the 50 and older crowd.

The benefits for senior singles is that you are never too old to find that special someone to connect and share your life with. Many seniors tend to isolate themselves as they get older, which can be harmful mentally and emotionally.

It is important that you reach out for positive relationships, make friends, and connect with those you share things in common with. You might even find your soulmate!

Precautions

There are some things to be on the lookout for when choosing a senior online dating website domestically and internationally.

Check out the reviews written about the site from other seniors. Make sure the comments are timely.

Do your comparative shopping and get the best price and value for the price the developers are asking for. Find at least five of the most popular senior dating websites to compare. I have included a list of senior-focused dating sites in the appendix.

Be sure that the websites require personality tests for their potential users. This measure will increase your chances of being matched with someone who shares the same interests, personality traits, values, and needs.

Most importantly, check out the safety and security tools the website has in place to protect its users from scammers, creepers, and con-artists. Make sure the website has added strategies to confirm the authenticity of its users.

Tips

Here are some tips for senior online daters:

Always be honest about yourself, especially with weight and height descriptions.

Do not be too transparent in laying all of your cards on the table right away.

Use a current profile photo and not one from years ago that does not show your true self.

Set realistic expectations and goals.

Choose a safe place to meet someone with whom you have communicated with online.

Tell someone in your immediate circle where you will be and with whom.

Have these people check on you often while on the date.

Never send money to anyone you've met online.

Be leery of dating site matches who refuse to meet in person or talk on the phone. This could be a sign that he or she is hiding something, like an existing relationship.

Be careful if a user you've been matched with comes across too strong and aggressive in professing his or her love for you right away.

Keep an open mind. This positive action to try online dating is supposed to be fun and satisfying!

Appendix A: Immigration Lawyers

I have compiled a shortlist of reputable immigration lawyers who were recommended to me personally. Please note that not a single one of them has paid for a mention in this book, and they receive no compensation for my mention here.

I simply aim to point you in the right direction as you venture into your international relationship.

The contact information is accurate as of the time of this publication and is subject to change. The best lawyer for you is one who is local to you, available, affordable, and competent. Most immigration lawyers will give you a free consultation, usually over the phone, before they decide to take your case.

Pamela Dru Sutton, Stone & Sutton, P.A. 837 Grace Avenue, Panama City, FL 32402 Call 850-250-5604
Nicole L. Goetz, P.L. 4933 Tamiami Trail N, Suite 201, Naples, FL 34103
Stone & Sutton, P.A. 837 Grace Avenue, Panama City, FL 32402 Call 850-250-5604
Mary Elizabeth Quinn, Esq., Quinn & Lynch, P.A. 412 st Madison Street, Suite 1008, Tampa, FL 33602 Call 813-955-8886
Rice Law Firm 222 Seabreeze Boulevard, Daytona Beach, FL

32118
Curry Law Group, P.A. 750 West Lumsden Road, Brandon, FL 33511-6217 Call 813-413-6074
Morris Law Group 7284 West Palmetto Park Road, Suite 101, Boca Raton, FL 33433
Law Office of Alecia Reading 20 S. Rose Avenue, Suite 8, Kissimmee, FL 34741 Call 407-966-3917
Law Offices of Lawrence S. Katz, P.A. 9130 South Dadeland Boulevard, Miami, FL 33156-7814 Call 305-424-9763
Law Offices of Grant J. Gisondo, P.A. 500 Village Square Crossing, Suite 103, Palm Beach Gardens, FL 33410 Free Consultation CALL 561-507-1966
Gregory S. Bloshinsky, B.C.S., Morris Law Group 7284 West Palmetto Park Road, Suite 101, Boca Raton, FL 33433 Free Consultations
STONE GRZEGOREK & GONZALEZ LLP | PARTNER Los Angeles 213-627-8997
BESHARA GLOBAL MIGRATION LAW FIRM | MANAGING PARTNER 555 Winderley Place, Suite 300 Orlando/Maitland, Florida 32751 P: (407) 571-6878 E: execadmin@besharapa.com
EB-5 PLUS IMMIGRATION LAW | ATTORNEY 433 N. Camden Drive, Suite 600, Beverly Hills, CA 90210 213-792-2325 BELMA@EB5PLUSIMMIGRATIONLAW.COM
DAVIES & ASSOCIATES LLC | CHAIRMAN mdavies@usimmigrationadvisor.com Phone: +1 (646) 201-5512 375 Park Avenue Suite 2607, 26th Floor New York, New York 10152
I.A. DONOSO & ASSOCIATES | FOUNDER 7401 WISCONSIN AVENUE, SUITE 400, BETHESDA MD 20814 301-276-0653
LAW OFFICES OF ROBERT P. GAFFNEY | ATTORNEY 601 Montgomery Street Suite 1114 San Francisco, CA 94111 Telephone: 415-503-9653
GREEN & SPIEGEL | ATTORNEY & EB-5 SECTION HEAD MGALATI@GANDS-US.COM 215-395-8959

FRAGOMEN | MANAGING PARTNER, FLORIDA OFFICE egonzalez@fragomen.com 800 NW 62ND AVENUE, MIAMI, FL 33126, UNITED STATES T +1 305 774 5800 F +1 305 774 6666
JENNIFER HERMANSKY Philadelphia 1-215-988-7800 hermanskyj@gtlaw.com 11111-1
MILLER MAYER | PARTNER 1-607-273-4200 info@millermayer.com
DAVID HIRSON & PARTNERS, LLP | MANAGING PARTNER 1-949-383-5369 info@hirsonimmigration.com

Appendix B: Dating Sites

These are the dating sites that I found during my research. I make no endorsements of these sites personally. They are provided for your purposes to decide which one you might want to utilize.

Weigh the costs, benefits, and procedures of these sites as you wish.

I would also caution against signing up for too many sites at once, as it might dilute your experience.

Match.com
Using its large user base, this site promises that you may find the match of your dreams there. This website is for users looking for a long relationship. This division of the website claims that everyone can fulfill their goals of success when it comes down to dating at whatever commitment level might be for the users.
3-months: $29.99/month, 6-months: $20.99/month, 12-months: $19.99/month

EliteSingles.com
EliteSingles caters to the mature person who is established,

roughly the 30-55 age range searching for a long-term serious relationship and who are college-educated.
Basic membership: Free, 3-months: $57.95/month, 6-months: $44.95/month, 12-months: $31.95/month

Zoosk.com
Zoosk claims to the best introvert dating website around. The site allows users to peruse its standard pickings of candidate profile matches with basic and advance search engines with the goal of finding a befitting connection. Zoosk.com promises users will find like-minded people of similar interests and compatibility.
1-month: $29.95/month, 3-months: $19.98/month, 6-months: $12.49/month

Eharmony.com
eHarmony is for the single who doesn't mind spending a few coins to get what he or she wants. When signing up, a user is almost immediately paired with available matches. The website offers a communication tool where singles can ask questions of other singles to jumpstart the potential connection.
3-months: $54.95/month, 6-months: $36.95/month, 12-months: $18.95/month

GamerDating.com
GamerDating, as its name implies, focuses solely on the avid gamer. This is with the gaming community in mind. Gamer prizes are given to all participants. The way the website matches up gamers is by posting their game history. This allows matches to see the games interested players have played in the library of games. This immediately informs the users what kind of games the profiler is into and a reason to start a conversation - shared interests.
Basic account: Free, 2-months: $35, 4-months: $70

iHookup.com
This website is for single who want casual interactions with other singles. This is for those who are not looking for a serious commitment, but one-night stands or friends with benefits. Usually, users upload photos of their faces for potential viewing by other interested parties.
Basic membership: Free, 1-month: $34.99, 3-months: $22.99/month, 12-months: $9.99/month

AdultFriendFinder.com
This website honestly touts itself to be for the down and dirty single. Its raunchy homepage is an indication of that being the case. There are also options available for the recreational

hookups. The website images seem to lean more on the slightly pornographic side compared to other dating websites. Users can use videos and participate in sexting. Use AFF to find an in-person rendezvous or get it on with people via sexting or raunchy videos.

Basic membership: Free, 1-month: $30/month, 3-months: $20/month, 12-months: $15/month

OkCupid

Ok Cupid's matchmaking goals are to make people open up about themselves to encourage the possibilities of finding the right person. General interests and lifestyle information are required. The website wants participants to provide honest and truthful information to other users of interest.

Basic subscription: Free, 1-month of A-List : $9.95/month, 3-months of A-List: $7.95/month, 6-months of A-List: $6.95/month

SoulGeek

This website praises the world of single geeks. It captures the essence for users of all shapes, sizes, and lifestyles. This is a place where members of the geek world can meet, socialize, and form romantic friendships. They can share their love of games and geek niches. This includes the geek culture in areas of comics and film.

Basic membership: Free, Membership with perks: $9.95/month

Cuddli

Cuddli is hailed as a place for the geek dater. It seeks to filter out catfishing and is like a Tinder or Bumblebee type of feel. A place where geeks and nerds can get together and socialize. It works along with the user's Facebook profile, basic information, and pictures. It encourages users to take their time when connecting with a potential match or matches.

Basic membership: Free, 1-month: $5, 3-months: $10, 6-months: $20, Lifetime membership: $50

Appendix C: Wedding Planners

My wedding planner was a real gem! She was perfect for me as we got along swimmingly. She understood my preferences, kept in contact with me, and had a calming, pleasing manner about her. She was wonderful, and I left her an online review to say so.

When searching for a wedding planner, you should find one that is, of course, affordable, but also understands your wants and needs and isn't trying to push his or her own preferences on you. The best wedding planner is local to you so she can be accessible for meeting you and also to utilize vendors in the local area.

I have also included a sample package price, so you can compare what the average wedding price is.

Fairytaleweddingsbymary.com, Package Price $2,295
A-One Weddings & Events.com, Package Price $1,200
Kiss The Planner.com, Package Price $5,000
An Affair to Remember by Sharon.com, Package Price $1,000

Gifted Events, Package Price $4,000
Smiling Through Chaos.com, Package Price $2,320
Coordinate Cuba.com, Package Price $1,435
Joyfully Blessed Events & Artistic Design.com, Package Price $800
Season Premiere LLC, Package Price $500
BlackTie+Lace, Package Price 1,500
Magnificent M. Iles Events, Package Price: $800
Completely Coordinated, Package Price $950
BW Studio + Events, Package Price $1,600
Ivory & Elm, Package Price $1,350
Designs by Ayanna, Package Price $3,500
Chic Dreams Events, Package Price $2,500

Appendix D: Foreign Matchmaking Services

Here is a list of some Foreign Matchmaking Services that I found while doing my research.

Aisha's Links (Aisha Matrimonial Service), (407) 350-8795, 1301 Amedoro Ct, Abingdon, MD 21009
Armed Forces Proxy Marriage, (406) 249-2095, Bigfork, MT 59911-6127
Ben's House of Mail Order Brides, (816) 752-3734, 1021 N Woodbine, Saint Joseph, MO 64504
Bharat Matrimony, 220 Davidson Ave, Ste 315, Somerset, NJ 08873
Containment Inc., (844) 818-0664, 815 N. Royal Str. Suite 202, Alexandria, VA 22314
A Foreign Affair, (602) 468-9111, 7227 N. 16th Street #240, Phoenix, AZ 85020-5239
A Foreign Affair, (602) 553-8178, 7320 N Dreamy Draw Dr Ste 200, Phoenix, AZ 85020-5362
Global Matri, (972) 840-3495, 3614 Columbia Boulevard, Garland, TX 75043
The Inspirations Company LLC, (866) 974-6453, 429 B Weber Road #288, Romeoville, IL 60446-3972

License Power Inc., (646) 932-8900, 333 E 45th St Apt 15D, New York, NY 10017
Marriage Quest, (802) 563-3063, 340 Deeper Ruts Rd, Cabot, VT 05647-9797
Matt Loter Justice of the Peace, (203) 524-5756, 81 Beacon Ave, New Haven, CT 06512-1970
Military Pay Proxy Marriage, (866) 627-1689, 270F N El Camino Real #120, Encinitas, CA 92024
Proxy Marriage - A Big Sky Event, (406) 249-5665, PO Box 9018, Kalispell, MT 59904-2018
Proxy Marriage-A Big Sky Event, (406) 249-5665, Kalispell, MT 59901
St. Louis Marriage Coaching, (314) 606-4272, 301 Summer Haven Ct, O Fallon, MO 63368-8090
A Volga Girl, (877) 297-5300, Prospect, KY 40059-7555
Luxury Matchmaking, 5775 Wayzata Blvd, Suite 700, St. Louis Park, Minnesota, 55416, Phone: (855) 622-8743, https://www.luxematchmaking.com
Selective Search, 35 East Wacker Drive, Suite 1920, Chicago, IL 60601, Phone: (866) 592-1200, https://www.selectivesearch.com
Janis Spindel & Carly Spindel – Serious Matchmaking, 745 Fifth Avenue, Suite 500, New York, New York 10151, Phone: (212) 987-1582, https://janisspindelmatchmaker.com
Kelleher International, San Francisco, CA 94104, Phone: (855) 207-4946, http://www.kelleher-international.com
Luma Search, 5775 Wayzata Blvd, Suite 700, St. Louis Park, Minnesota, 55416, Phone: (855) 622-8743,

https://www.luxematchmaking.com

Amy Laurent, 590 Madison Avenue, 21st Floor, New York, NY 10022, Phone: (866) 601-3737, http://www.amylaurent.com

Appendix E: Resources for Support

While you're on this journey of your international relationship, you should seek some assistance and support. Here is a list of forums and websites where you can meet and chat about your situation.

International Marriage and Relationships, https://www.internations.org
Long Distance Relationship Forum, members.lovingfromadistance.com
Marriage Forum at Marriage.com, https://www.marriage.com › forum
International Association of Marriage and Family Counselors, www.iamfconline.org
www.multilingualliving.com
Couples Resorts Message Board, https://mb.couples.com
Relationships Forum, https://www.city-data.com/forum
K-1 Fiancé(e) Visa Process & Procedures, https://www.visajourney.com
Landmark Forum, www.landmarkworldwide.com
OnCourse International, https://www.oncourseinternational.com › family-couples

STMA Breakfast Forum, https://www.couplesforchristglobal.org
Couples Alive Forum International, https://www.vconnect.com
Season 2 Discussion - 90 Day Fiancé - PRIMETIMER - Forums – PRIMETIMER, https://forums.primetimer.com
International couple — The Knot Community, https://forums.theknot.com
Marriage in crisis forum, www.soales.it › marriage-in-crisis-forum
Wedding Wire Forums, https://www.weddingwire.com/wedding-forums
International Couples - Delphi Forums Index, forums.delphiforums.com
Forum about International Marriage, https://community.travelchinaguide.com/international-marriage

Appendix F: LBGTQ Dating Sites

HER is a free website that caters to the lesbian woman. The website is made by queer women for queer women. It goes a step further in offering LGBT events and news as an added bonus to its active user community. HER is free to download, and there are no fees attached to any app purchases.

EliteSingle.com

Claims to separate itself from the other websites with its "intelligent matchmaking" where users are curated and supported by an in-house team. Users are 85% well-educated, and 100% vetted. Users are also sorted by test scores, location, income levels, and education. With these odds, a user is sure to find a same-sex love match.

OkCupid.com

This website uses advanced matchmaking technology and in-depth questionnaires to pair users together. OkCupid also has an extensive dating pool and social media following. OkCupid developers offer expanded gender and sexual orientation options. It is being touted as the first real dating website comes with a trusted name and huge lesbian following.

Basic account that includes messaging: Free, A-List Basic: $4.95/month, A-List Premium: $19.90/month

Plenty Of Fish.com

Criteria relies almost entirely on questionnaires to aid users in finding a partner you have chemistry with. Dating website that claims to be inclusive of all sexual orientations.

Basic memberships are free, Premium membership starts at $7 a month.

FEM.com

Meet eligible lesbians through videos to combat against being catfished, requiring Facebook approval to avoid these horror stories. An online platform uses videos instead of profile pictures as an added measure of protection and safety. FEM is free to download and there are no additional fees for app purchases

Hinge.com

This site describes itself as the "relationship app" or the anti-Tinder. Founders of the website use Facebook and will only match you with a friend of friends solely. The website promises to accept users of all sexual orientations. Hinge.com is free to download and for unlimited matches, there's a cost of $7 a month to upgrade.

OneScene.com

This refers to itself as an international LGBT community that offers easy registration and matches for the gay, lesbian, bisexual, transgender, fluid, questioning singles. The website even goes a step further in assisting newcomers with tips, updating their profiles, photos, and how to manage their accounts. This is a free service that the website organizers offer.

BeNaughty.com

This is a website that concentrates on hookups, chats, location, and encounters for lesbian women. The website is free to use and several search filters for hookups and chat. The website gets 13.3 million visits a month.

Grindr.com

Began in 2009 and deemed itself as the gay dating app that trumps all LBGT websites. This is a male-only website that moves fast from "how are you?" to "when can we meet" in a matter of minutes. The app particularly caters to single men who live in your area for a hookup. There is a free version with advertisements. Grindr Xtra is a paid subscription that costs from $12 to $60, depending on the plan selected.

Appendix G: LGBT Advocacy Groups

Here is a listing of some support and advocacy organizations that provide services to LGBT people globally, regionally, locally, and statewide. It is always a good practice to connect with advocacy and support organizations that may be able to assist or solve professional, social, legal, or economic issues faced by these special populations as well as mainstream communities.

Louisiana Trans Advocates-lends support to the transgender population across Louisiana through social supports, education, empowerment and advocacy.

Alaskans Together For Equity is Alaska's statewide awareness and advocacy group, which caters to bisexual and transgender Alaskans.

Anti-Violence Project - AVP works to empower lesbian, gay, bisexual, transgender, queer, and HIV-affected communities to end all forms of violence by way of education, organizing and other supports.

Basic Rights Oregon concentrates on ensuring lesbian, gay, bisexual, and transgender Oregonians receive fairness in building a broad politically powerful movement.

CenterLink's aim is to support a strong, sustainable LGBT community that centers around a unified movement.

COLAGE brings together lesbian, gay, bisexual, transgender, and queer parents to a network of peers who work together as they mature and empower each other.

Equality Alabama's mission is to advocate equality for the LGBT community where they live, work, and play through education and advocacy.

Equity Arizona's mission is to advocate for the LGBT community where they live, work, and play through education and advocacy.

Equity California's mission is to advocate for the LGBT community where they live, work and play through education and advocacy.

Equity Florida's mission is to advocate for the LGBT community where they live, work, and play through education and advocacy.

Equity Hawai'i's mission is to advocate for the LGBT community where they live, work, and play through education and advocacy.

Equality Federation builds strategic partners with US-state-based organizations advancing equality for LGBT communities where they live.

All Out mobilizes millions of people to build a world where no one will have to sacrifice their family and freedom for safety and dignity because of who they are.

Amnesty International is a global organization comprised of 3 million supporters, activists, and members in more than 150 countries and territories who campaign to end abuse.

Bi Social Network (BSN) works primarily with underserved communities on poverty issues, teen homelessness, marginalized groups, and the elderly.

Diversity PRO is a Non-Government Organization (NGO) working to raise awareness of workplace diversity and inclusion, advocating diversity in leadership.

Equaldex is a collaborative knowledge database geared towards the LGBT movement. The organization crowdsources law-related LGBT rights to produce a comprehensive global view.

Freedom to Marry was started in 2003 by Evan Wolfson, known as the civil rights attorney considered as the architect of the national marriage-equity movement.

Global Action for Trans Equality (GATE) is a trans network coordinator, facilitator, and advocate to the "outside" world and works to unite trans movements for common goals.

GRIN Campaign unites globally to up against bullying, particularly against lesbian, gay, bisexual, transgender, and queer communities.

ILGA-Europe is the European area for the International lesbian, gay, bisexual, Trans, and Intersex Association that works for equality and human rights for the lesbian, gay, bisexual and transgender population.

It Gets Better Project's aim is to communicate to lesbian, gay, bisexual, and transgender youth around the world that it gets better and to create and inspire changes.

Appendix H: Dating Sites for the Older Single

SeniorFriendsDate.com

SeniorFriendsDate is a senior dating site with a diverse international network. This site allows people of all ages to join, but it caters to seniors who want to build genuine relationships. It is free to join, but to get premium features there is a cost.

Senior FriendFinder.com

Senior FriendFinder is targeted towards to more adventurous older audience. It also gives options to choose like a woman, man, couple, or group. Free version: Yes, 1-month silver: $22.95/month, 3-months silver: $11.95/month, 1-month gold: $34.95/month, 3-months gold: $14.98/month

SeniorMatch.com

Senior Match.com believes a person needs to have a companion to share their lives and experiences with. This could be a romantic interest or simply a friendship. Free version: Yes

50Plus Club.com

The 50 Plus Club is a strictly 50 and over dating website. Registered users can find partners for dating, companionship, and join in on discussions. Seniors can get to know other like-minded people. Cost: Free

Age Match.com

This website operates a little differently where it matches up older singles with younger matches. AgeMatch.com believes that age is nothing but a number and that age differences are less important than finding that special someone to spend quality time with. Cost: Free when you first join, $29.95 a month to upgrade to Gold membership.

Conclusion

Long-distance relationships in themselves can be tenuous, regardless of the fact that your partner is a foreign national. If your love can traverse the barriers of timezones, language, and culture, then it was truly meant to be!

I hope that you can find love and happiness, just as Hon and I have. I really never thought that a simple, good-natured dare from some mischievous coworkers would lead to me actually finding my soulmate.

After my sordid past with boyfriends whom I had met in person in various ways, I feel like all that experience just paved the way for me to meet the man of my dreams!

If this book has helped you or inspired you in any way, would you please consider leaving a review about this book wherever you happen to have purchased it?

Reviews help to get this book in the hands of even more people who need support and guidance in the area of international relationships. I want to provide them with answers and hope, just as I wish for you, too.

Best of luck with your endeavors!